Those not yet familiar with
meditational practice and
Chinese wisdom will find
this book a guide to teachings
which have influenced Eastern
civilization for thousands of
years.

The concepts are presented
simply, with the aim of
introducing new students
to the age-old peaceful art
of meditation as practiced
by sages of the past and
present.

KUNG FU

MEDITATIONS

&
CHINESE PROVERBIAL WISDOM

Selections adapted by **ELLEN KEI HUA**
Calligraphy & illustrations by **MAKY**

for Bill + Lil —
May the Cosmic
Light illuminate your
path + fill your lives
with Rainbow light.

Love —

Laura

Library of Congress Cataloging in Publication Data

Hua, Ellen Kei, 1945–
    Kung Fu meditations & Chinese proverbial wisdom.

    1. Meditations. 2. Proverbs, Chinese. I. Title.
BL1810.H83   181'.11   73-7731

KUNG FU MEDITATIONS &
CHINESE PROVERBIAL WISDOM

First Edition: June 1973
Second Printing: July 1973
Third Printing: August 1973
Fourth Printing: September 1973
Fifth Printing: November 1973
Sixth Printing: January 1974

A FAROUT PRESS BOOK

Manuscript prepared
under the supervision of
Laura D'Auri

FAROUT PRESS BOOKS
Thor Publishing Company   Printed in the
P O Box 1782   Ventura   United States
California   93001   of America

Also by Ellen Kei Hua and
illustrated by Maky:

WISDOM FROM THE EAST:
Meditations, Reflections,
Proverbs & Chants

A violent man shall die a violent death.
This will be the essence of the teaching.

The aim of meditation is to achieve peace of mind and a quiet spirit.

Meditation is not generally connected with any physical exercise or activity but meditation can help you in your studies by putting your mind in a receptive state.

Meditation exercise is a way of life for many thousands of people in China and throughout the East. Kung fu is also practiced by many people and in most of the small villages in China the entire population still gathers in the main square every morning to practice the tai chi forms together for health of body and peace of spirit.

This book has been prepared for those of you who wish to practice kung fu and tai chi and who are interested in meditation.

This guide can be used alone as a beginner's book
of meditation, or it can be used in conjunction
with Bruce Tegner's book of kung fu and tai chi*
as an aid to learning the forms. Kung fu forms
are basically for exercise. The first part of this
book is intended to help you gather your concentration in order to prepare for learning the forms,
but there are no direct page references because
this is an auxiliary or optional procedure.

Tai chi, as well as being an exercise in control,
concentration and grace of movement, has deep
symbolic meaning. In the tai chi meditation
section of this book, you will find page references
to the forms outlined in Bruce Tegner's book,
which have been correlated (when applicable)
to symbolic parallels in some of the Chinese
phrases. Notes and commentary will be found
on the left hand pages, with the teachings on
the right hand pages.

Before you learn an art, it is a "secret." When
the Chinese refer to "secrets" they do not mean
it in the sense that we use the word in our
Western culture. By secrets, they mean the
unknown. When you are in a state of mind
capable of perceiving the "secrets" (the
unknown), they shall be revealed to you. When
you are in a state of meditation, you will learn
the forms more easily and you will remember
them better.

*Bruce Tegner's Book of Kung Fu and Tai Chi:
Chinese Karate and Classical Exercises, Thor
Publishing Co., Ventura, Calif. 93001

HOW TO BEGIN MEDITATION

To begin meditation, you must first find a quiet place where you can block out as much noise as possible. If you are in the country, an outdoor area is ideal, or choose the quietest place you can at home.

The lotus position is not recommended for beginners as your limbs would feel the strain and perhaps deter you from your meditation. Start with a cross-legged Indian position with your back straight and your hands resting lightly, palms up, on your thighs; or, you may sit on a straight-backed chair with your feet flat on the floor if this is more comfortable. You should be in a level area: if you are outdoors, the grass or earth will make a comfortable blanket; if you are sitting on the floor, you should sit on a rug or mat.

When beginning meditation exercises, you must try to rid your mind of any thoughts and concentrate solely on the particular meditation aid you have chosen. At first you may find this difficult, as your mind will start to wander into a multitude of worldly thoughts such as, "What am I going to have for dinner?", "I wonder if it is going to rain", "Did I lock my car?" Do not feel frustrated during your first attempts at meditation, as this is contrary to the practice itself. Each time you find yourself wandering from your meditation, note where your thoughts are going and return to the practice at hand. To relax, you may start with a breathing exercise: inhale to a count of 20, hold to a count of 20, exhale to a count of 20. NOTE: Never hold your breath to the point of strain.

Read the meditation exercise. Repeat the words
to yourself slowly several times. (You should be
in the meditation position.) Close your eyes and
meditate upon the meaning of the words. Try to
meditate and remain in that state for several
minutes at the beginning, increasing the time span
as you feel you are able. You will find that the
more you meditate, the easier it becomes.

You have no doubt heard of enlightened Eastern
masters who spend most of their lives in caves
in deep meditation without uttering a word to
anyone. This way of being is not available to
nor perhaps desirable for most of you and it takes
many years to reach this high state of meditation.
You must not feel that you will receive instant
illumination by meditating, but daily meditation
practice can help anyone to achieve peace of mind.
This in turn will aid you in ridding yourself of
negative thoughts and the frustration of daily life,
because things cease to be frustrating and annoying
when your mind is peaceful. The aim of any
meditational practice is to help the student gain
peace of mind and self-knowledge and whichever
method helps the individual to attain that goal is
right for that person.

In addition to the meditation aids in this book,
some other beginning and effective meditation
practices are: concentration on a single sound,
such as the ring of a bell, or enunciation of a
sound such as OM (or "aum": the mystic
equivalent for the name of God, also symbolizing
the triple constitution of the cosmos; the absolute,

the relative, and the relation between them. It
has been adopted by modern occultists to denote
absolute goodness and spiritual truth.) OM can
either be pronounced aloud or thought silently
and is universally used in meditation practice.

When employing the sound of a bell, ring the bell
once and meditate on the sound it makes, following
the sound into infinity. When using OM, think or
say the word to yourself, drawing out the syllable,
and follow and meditate on this sound. You can
meditate on anything that keeps other thoughts
out of your head; the sound of rain, the sound of
wind, the song of a bird. The idea of these aids
is that after awhile the meditation on these sounds
will rid your mind of thoughts and you will not
need the sound but will remain in a peaceful
no-mind state.

No-Mind

The concept of no-mind is difficult for a
Westerner to comprehend because we have been
conditioned to think that we must always have
thoughts in our minds. No-mind means that you
are free of worldly thoughts and that your mind
and spirit are free floating and are one with the
Universal Consciousness. No-mind is universally
accepted throughout the East and many individuals-
businessmen, professionals and working people -
spend time daily in meditational no-mind practice.

THE TEACHINGS

You will find many references to the "Tao" (pronounced "dow") in the pages to follow. The "tao" means the Way. All meditation and spiritual exercise leads to the Way. The Way does not refer to peace only during meditational practice; it applies to peace in your general outlook when dealing with daily life. When you have found the Way you can find peace in all things. Violence and hostility shall disappear from your being, to be replaced by love for all things.

The teachings of the tao are to be found in the Tao Te Ching by Lao Tze (an older Chinese contemporary of Confucious) and in the book of Chuang-Tsu, as well as the works of many lesser known sages. Many of the teachings from the Tao Te Ching will be found in this book. Also incorporated are phrases, sayings, and lessons from other Chinese and Eastern sages, and from the I Ching (Book of Changes), which was a common source for both Confucianist and Taoist philosophy and which is still consulted today.

For those of you unfamiliar with Chinese sayings and philosophy, some of them may seem difficult to understand: so do not try to understand them; meditate on them. Much of the vagueness in the Chinese phrases is due to the difficulty of turning the vagueness of Chinese literature into the definiteness of English thought. At best, language can never be more than an imperfect method of transmitting thoughts to the brains of others. And in the Chinese language, one character can stand for several different things and can be used interchangeably as a noun, verb and adjective. Therefore, several different meanings can be inferred from each phrase and it is left to the translator's discretion to convey the value and meaning of the phrase.

So, read the thoughts and meditate upon them. Read them over and over until the words flow effortlessly through your head. The meanings will be unveiled to you when you are ready to receive them; probably when you least expect it.

The Way is to find meditation and peace in everything you do, be it mowing the lawn, playing an instrument, washing the dishes, looking at the stars, building a house. As long as you find yourself doing that particular thing, you might as well enjoy it. Do not think of what you could be doing. Think of what you are doing and find peace in it. Doing this you find peace within yourself. This is the aim of all meditational practice.

COMMENTARY: In lines 4 and 5, "...ten
thousand things" is the symbolic reference to
all things in the cosmos.

Lines 5 and 6 refer to the Chinese principle of
yin/yang (positive/negative), the symbol of
which is illustrated above and on the cover.
The yin is the negative principle, receptive,
passive. The yang is the complement, positive,
active and aggressive. From the constant
interaction, blending and harmony of these
forces, all phenomena emerge. The yin and
yang alternate, so that one is dominant while
the other is recessive.

MEDITATION 1

Tao gives birth to one.
One gives birth to two.
Two gives birth to three.
Three gives birth to ten thousand things.

Ten thousand things find harmony
by combining the forces of
positive and negative.

A violent man will die a violent death.
That will be the essence of the teaching.

COMMENTARY: "...embraces the one" refers to embracing the Tao (One), meaning following the Way. When you are truly one with the Tao, your every act will be wise and true and you will have no need to "prove" yourself in the eyes of others.

MEDITATION 2

The wise person embraces the one and
sets an example to all.
Not putting on a show,
he shines;
not justifying himself,
he is distinguished;
not bragging,
he receives recognition.

He does not quarrel,
so no one quarrels with him.

MEDITATION 3

We barely know that which is highest.

We know that which we love,
that which we fear,
and that which we despise.

Who does not trust enough
will not be trusted.

He
    who
        knows
            others

is wise.

He
    who
        knows
            himself

is enlightened.

MEDITATION 5

Who has little shall receive.
Who has much shall be embarrassed.

MEDITATION 6

Those who know honor
but practice humility
will be as a valley
receiving all the world into it

MEDITATION 7

Achieve, but do not glory in the results.
Achieve, but do not boast of the results.
Achieve results, but not through violence.
Force is followed by loss of strength.

MEDITATION 8

The Way is sacred; you cannot own it.
He who would win it would destroy it.
He who would hold it would lose it.

You will find, therefore, that
sometimes things are ahead
and sometimes they are behind.

Sometimes there will be strength and
sometimes there will be weakness.

Thus, the sage avoids extremes, indulgence,
and complacency

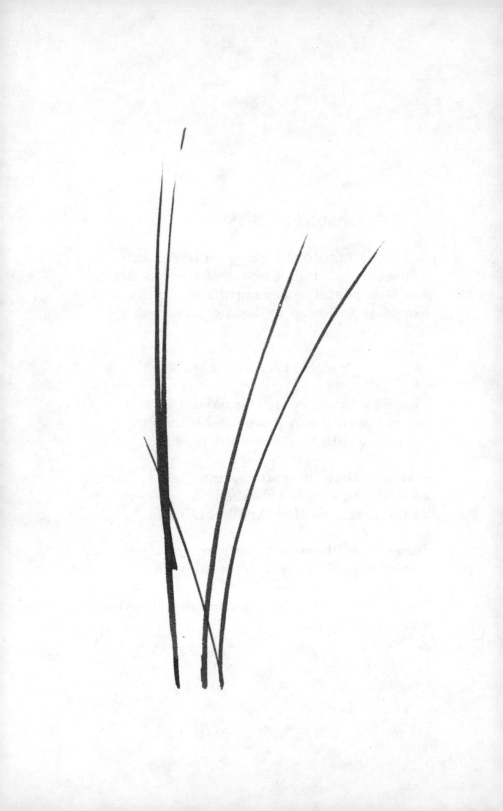

The Master Carpenter Chang presented a
carved wooden music stand to the prince
of the region. When looked upon by the
people, they declared it to be of supernatural
execution. When questioned by the prince,
Chang replied, "There is no mystery, your
Grace, and yet here is the manner in which
it was prepared."

"When I commence my task, I am intent on
the preservation of my vital powers. I rid
my mind of all thoughts until it is quiet as
a silent pool. After three days, all thoughts
of rewards to be gained have passed. After
five days, I am oblivious of any fame which
might become mine. Seven days pass and I
no longer feel my body. It is then I go into
the forest, when all disturbing elements
from without are gone and my skill is my
concentration. The suitable tree appears
to me, in the form required, and I set about
creating that which I see in my mind's eye.
My own natural skills are brought into
harmony with the nature of the wood. That
which was thought to be supernatural execution
is due only to this."

MEDITATION 10

Understanding comes to those
who have realized their true Self.

Realization of their true Self
comes to those who have gained
understanding.

MEDITATION 11

To him who has reached the Tao and is
master of his true Self, the universe
shall be dissolved.

Should he find himself in the company of
loud and aggressive persons, he is like
a lotus flower growing in muddy water;
touched but not soiled.

MEDITATION 12

With deep Self-realization, a person influences
the universe with his subtle vibrations, and is
less affected by the flow of events.

MEDITATION 13

Those who attain Self-realization on earth
live a double existence. They perform their
worldly duties conscientiously, but are inwardly
immersed in spiritual peace.

MEDITATION 14

Human life is full of sorrow, until we know
of the Way, whose "right course" may be
confusing to the egotistic intelligence.

MEDITATION 15

To reach the goal of perfect peace
empty yourself of all things.
All in nature stands before your eyes.
The ten thousand things grow and flourish,
and then return to the Source,
regaining perfect peace.
This is the way of Nature:
the way of Nature is unchanging.

He is enlightened who has learned this well.
And he who knows of it will be tolerant;
and being tolerant is therefore just.

Being just you will have an open mind.
With an open mind you will be open-hearted.
Being open-hearted you will act with grace.
With open mind and open heart and acts of
grace, you will attain the divine.

Being divine, you will be at one with the Tao.
Being at one with the Tao is eternal.
And though the body dies, the Tao
will never pass away.

MEDITATION 16

In dwelling, be close to the land.
In meditation, delve deep into the heart.
In dealing with others, be gentle and kind.
In speech, be true.
In work, be competent.
In action, be careful of your timing.

Where there is no fight
there is no blame.

MEDITATION 17

Only do what needs to be done.
Do not take advantage of power.
Counsel others not to use force
to conquer the universe.
This only brings resistance.
And thorn bushes spring up
when the army has passed.

MEDITATION 18

Knowing others is wisdom.
Knowing the Self is enlightenment.

He who overcomes others is strong.
He who overcomes himself is mighty.

He who knows he has enough is rich.
He who stays where he is endures.
Perseverance is an attribute of the will.

To die but not to perish
is to be eternally present.

MEDITATION 19

Without going outside the door,
one understands all that takes place
under the sky.

Without looking through the window,
one sees the way of the Tao.

The farther one goes out from the Self,
the less one knows.

The sage knows without traveling.
He sees without looking.
He works without doing.

MEDITATION 20

Many spokes unite to form the wheel
but it is the center that makes it useful.
When you shape clay into an urn,
it is the space within that makes it useful.
Cut doors and windows in a room;
the openings make them useful.

From the material, comes profit.
From the immaterial, usefulness.

MEDITATION 21

Ten thousand things
cease not to rise and fall.
Creating, not possessing.
Working, not taking credit.
Work is done, then forgotten.
Therefore it lasts forever.

MEDITATION 22

Confucious said: Love

MEDITATION 23

He who knows that enough is enough
will always have enough.

MEDITATION 24

Man follows the earth
Earth follows heaven
Heaven follows the Tao
Tao follows what is natural

MEDITATION 25

The greatest object
of the Superior Person
is to preserve peace & tranquility.

He takes no pleasure
in winning battles
for if he did so
he would be finding gratification
in the pain of others.

He believes
that he who takes delight
in the defeat of others
does not follow the Tao.

That which is not the way of the Tao
will not endure.

COMMENTARY: Above is the Chinese
character for 'Peace' and the corresponding
hexagram as outlined in the I Ching or Book
of Changes. (For further commentary on
the hexagrams, consult the I Ching itself.)

In Meditation 26, 'hold fast to the center'
refers to our center of peace and tranquility
which each of us has and which we seek to
maintain by the practice of meditation.

MEDITATION 26

Heaven and Earth are like a bellows,
which seems empty when at rest
but when set in motion
contains an endless stream of air.

Not so with words, for much talking
leads to exhaustion.

Hold fast to the center.

MEDITATION 27

If one is determined in his efforts to
seek out the Tao, he may have residence
in the city and may hold high rank
in the eyes of men; this is not a conflict.
The work is easy and not so far away.
If the secret were to be disclosed,
it would be so simple that laughter
would be heard everywhere.

MEDITATION 28

It would seem that favor and disgrace
are both to be equally feared.
Honor and disaster must be regarded
as personal conditions of the same kind.

What do we mean by speaking thus
of favor and disgrace?
Disgrace is being in a lowly position
after having enjoyed favor.
Receiving favor leads
to apprehension of losing it;
Losing it leads to the fear
of still great disaster.
Therefore, favor and disgrace
are both to be equally feared.

And what do we mean by saying
that honor and disaster
are to be similarly regarded
as personal conditions?
Honor and disaster come
from having a body.
Without a body, how could they occur?

Surrender yourself humbly,
it is then you can care for all things.
Love the world as your Self,
it is then you may be truly entrusted
with all things.

MEDITATION 29

To return is the motion of the Tao.
To yield is the way of the Tao.
Ten thousand things are born of being.
Being is born of not being.

MEDITATION 30

Not caring for anyone in particular
is caring for all mankind in general.

****

MEDITATION 31

If, in order to practice charity
and duty to others, the Tao is set aside,
the sage has made an error.

****

MEDITATION 32

To go wrong and not to alter one's course
can definitely be defined as going wrong.

MEDITATION 33

A Chinese student was traveling in the
mountains and came upon a tree so large
that his surprise knew no limits.

How is it that this tree has grown so large?
As he looked, he saw that the branches were
crooked, thereby unable to provide a strong
roof.   The trunk had grown with such
irregularity that it would be spurned by
cabinetmakers.   The leaves were the
most bitter he had ever tasted; the odor
so heavy as to repel the strongest man.

Ah, he exclaimed, this tree would be deemed
useless by men and thus it has continued to
this size.   A good example for wise men to
follow.

MEDITATION 34

Forward and backward, abyss after abyss.
When in danger like this, pause first and wait.
Otherwise you will fall into the abyss.
Do not act in this manner.

MEDITATION 35

Those which are called the great glories
of the world take place in the twinkling
of an eye and pass away.

***

MEDITATION 36

When perceiving the Wonderful, one
knows not whether art is Tao or
Tao is art.

***

MEDITATION 37

Music in the soul can be heard by the universe.

***

MEDITATION 38

What can be the difference between
a so-called long life and a short one?
It is, after all, only a moment in
the infinity of time.

MEDITATION 39

Only those who leisurely approach
that which the masses are busy about
can be busy about
that which the masses take leisurely.

MEDITATION 40

While some advance
The rest retire
While some inhale
The rest respire
While some are weak
The rest are strong
While some stand still
The rest move on

MEDITATION 41

I dreamt I was a butterfly, fluttering
here and there. I followed only my actions
as a butterfly, and was not conscious
of being an individual. Then I found myself
awake, once more in my body. Was I a
person dreaming about being a butterfly
or am I a butterfly dreaming that I am
a person? There is necessarily a distinction
between a butterfly and a person. This
transition is called the transformation of
material things.

NOTE: Page number references in this section refer to Bruce Tegner's Book of Kung Fu and Tai Chi: Chinese Karate and Classical Exercises. When using this book by itself, you may disregard the page references.

COMMENTARY: The Great Circle (p. 92). The movements of the Great Circle are the first forms illustrated in the tai chi section of Bruce Tegner's book. The Great Circle also means the entire sequence (108 moves) of tai chi movements. The first five movements are used as a replenishing exercise and breathing exercise. They are symbolic of refurbishing the soul, attaining calmness. They are the key to focusing your attention on what you are doing. When the breath is controlled and regular, it regulates all your bodily functions.

FURTHER MEDITATIONS, with references
to the Great Circle of Tai Chi Movements.

ONE

What the world calls repose, the sage does not.
His repose derives from his mental attitude.
It becomes the mirror of the universe.
Nothing disturbs his tranquility.
Hence his repose.

CHUN
DIFFICULTY AT
THE BEGINING

COMMENTARY: To Touch the South Wind (p. 92)
This movement is symbolic of facing the
direction from which danger may come; to
show your strength to that direction. It shows
your readiness to defend, not to be the
aggressor.

TWO

It is natural to talk but little.
The high wind does not last all morning.
Neither does a sudden rain last all day.
Heaven and earth are not able
to make things last forever.
So how is it possible for man?

THREE

With only a little sense
you will walk on the main road.
The only fear will be
straying from it.
It is easy to stay on the main road.
But people seem to love
being led astray.

COMMENTARY: Touch the East Wind (p. 94)
This is symbolic of reaching out to touch the
spiritual truth, the Way.

FOUR

He who follows the Tao
is at one with the Tao.
If you lose the way,
you feel lost.
When you are one with the Tao,
you are welcomed.
When you are one with loss
the loss doesn't matter.

COMMENTARY: The Tide Comes In and Out
(p. 94).
These movements are symbolic of giving way,
overcoming. The gestures indicate that when
the onslaught comes, you flow back; when the
onslaught recedes, you flow back upon it.

FIVE

Tao in the world
is like the river flowing home
to the sea.

The great Tao flows everywhere.
Ten thousand things depend on it.
It silently fulfills its purpose;
it makes no claim.
It nourishes ten thousand things
and passes on in constant flow.
Passing on it becomes remote.
Having become remote, it returns.
It has no aim; it is very small.
Ten thousand things return to it.
Yet it is not their master.
It is very great
but does not show greatness.
Therefore it is truly great.

SIX

Conserve your power.
Be like the expansive ocean,
which absorbs quietly the
tributary rivers of the senses.

Cravings of the senses deplete
your inner peace;
they are like openings
in a reservoir
through which vital waters are wasted
in the barren soil of material things.
The urge of wrong desire
is the greatest enemy of happiness.

SEVEN

Of fame or life
which do you hold more dear?
Of life or wealth,
to which would you adhere?
Keep life and lose the other things;
keep them and lose your life -
which brings sorrow and pain more near?

Thus we may see
who clings to fame
rejects what is more great.
Who loves large stores
gives up the richer state.

Who is content
need fear no shame.
Who knows to stop
incurs no blame.
From danger free
long live shall he.

TA KUO
PREPONDERANCE OF THE GREAT

EIGHT

One must call upon the great
Tao if he is to bring relief
from the wrong manner of
living, or he shall lose his
chance and shall not be
regarded as a wise man.

A hundred years of life is
like the blink of an eye.
Those who seek only material
gain, fame and title, will see
their own pale faces and the
degeneration of their bodies.

Perhaps material things
can fill the valleys; these
possessions, however, are
non-permanent and cannot
buy the things which do not
come back.

Bird Perching (p. 96).
This gesture mimicks the actions of a
bird. It may be a rest position, passive;
or it may be defensive. A bird attacks
only upon the approach of danger.
Conserve your powers until such time
as they are needed.

NINE

When the Tao is present
in the universe,
the birds sing.

When the Tao is absent
from the universe,
the birds run from the
sounds of war.
Desire is not in keeping
with the Tao.
Discontent is a curse.
Misfortune is wanting things
for oneself.

He who know that enough
is enough
will always have enough

TEN

If you are offended by a quality
in your superiors,
do not behave in such a manner
to those below you.
If you dislike a quality
in those below you,
do not reflect that quality
to those who work over you.
If something bothers you
from the man at your heels,
do not push
at the one in front of you.

ELEVEN

He who stands on the tips of his toes
cannot be steady.
He who takes long strides
will not maintain the pace.
He who displays himself
is not enlightened.
He who brags
achieves nothing of worth.
He who boasts
will not endure.

These people do not bring happiness.
Followers of the Tao avoid them.

TWELVE

The superior man
when he stands alone
is without fear.

If he must renounce the world,
it does not matter.

Face The Wind (p. 100).
Facing the wind is symbolic of facing
that which may bring danger, fighting
greater odds. When confronting danger,
once you have made your decision,
follow through with smooth, controlled
action.

THIRTEEN

If there is something you have not studied,
or, having studied it you are unable to do it,
do not file it away; if there is a question
that you have not asked or to which
you have been unable to find the answer,
do not consider the matter closed;
if you have not thought of a problem,
or, having thought of it,
you have not resolved it,
do not think the matter settled;
if you have tried to make a distinction
but have not made it clear,
do not sink into contentment;
if there is a principle which
you have been unable to put into practice,
do not let up.
If one man gets there with one try,
try ten times.
If another succeeds with a hundred tries,
make a thousand.

Proceeding in this manner, even one
who is a bit slow will find the light,
even a weak man will find energy.

FOURTEEN

Knowing ignorance is strength.
Ignoring knowledge is disease.
By being pained at the thought
of having the disease,
we are preserved from it.

The sage does not have the disease.
He knows the pain that
would be inseparable from it
and therefore does not have it.

The Sun Wheel (p. 102).
These gestures are symbolic of
the sun, the source of light and energy.
This movement is done facing the East,
the source of spiritual truth.

FIFTEEN

When the dark seeks
to equal the light
there is certain to be a struggle.
If the dark element
seeks to maintain a position
to which it is not entitled
and to rule instead of serving,
it draws down upon itself
the anger of the dragon. *

* the dragon is the symbol
of heaven

SIXTEEN

The wise man seeks everything in himself;
the ignorant man tries to get everything
from somebody else.

- - - -

He who puts forth his strength
and keeps back his weakness,
is like a deep river
into which all the streams flow.

His virtues shall not wane
until he is
once more
as pure as in childhood.

小畜

䷈

SEVENTEEN

Modesty brings success.
It is the way of heaven to shine its light
downward to create radiance.
It is the way of earth to move ever upward.
It is the way of heaven to fill the empty
and increase the modest.
Spirits and gods bring harm to what is full
and prosperity to what is modest.
It is the way of men to hate fullness
and to love the modest.
Modesty spreads radiance.
Modesty cannot be ignored.
This is the end attained by the superior man.

A Bird with Folded Wing (p. 104).
A bird with folded wing is symbolic
of containing your inner peace
and powers; appraisal of the situation.

EIGHTEEN

When inner shock is at its height,
it robs a man of reflection
and clarity of vision.
In such a state of mind,
it is of course impossible
to act with presence of mind.
Then the right thing
is to keep still
until composure is regained.

But one can only do this
when he himself
is not yet affected by the agitation,
although its disastrous effects
are already visible in those around him.
If he withdraws from the matter in time,
he remains free of mistakes.

But his comrades,
who no longer pay attention to warning,
will, in their excitement,
certainly be displeased with him.

However,
he must not take this into account.

解

DELIVERANCE

NINETEEN

A vain nature invites diverting pleasures
and must suffer accordingly.
If a man is unstable within,
he does not shun the pleasures of the world,
and thus they have an influence so powerful
he is swept along by them.
Here it is no longer a question of danger,
of good fortune or misfortune.
He has given up direction of his own life,
and what becomes of him
depends upon chance and external influences.

TWENTY

Turning to the summit for nourishment,
Deviating from the path
To seek nourishment from the hill.
To continue to do this brings misfortune.

****

Divine contemplation
must not be made an excuse
for material carelessness.

TWENTY ONE

There is thunder within the earth.
Thus the kings of antiquity
closed the passes
at the time of solstice.
Merchants and strangers
did not go about.
And the ruler
did not travel through the provinces.

TWENTY TWO

The Tao of heaven is this:
to take from those
who have more than enough
and give to those
who do not have enough.

Man's way is different.
It is this:
to take from those
who do not have enough,
to give to those
who already have too much.

Is there a man
who has more than enough
and gives it away?
Only the man of Tao.

TWENTY THREE

The Tao is an empty vessel.
It is used, but never filled.
Unfathomable ancestor
of ten thousand things.
Blunt the sharp points,
unravel the knots,
soften the glare,
merge with the dust.

Hidden deep but ever present.

I do not know from whence it comes.
It might appear
to have always been here.

Defy the Dragon, Defy the Leopard,
Defy the Panther (110-112).
This is defined as presenting a
strong front - neither attacking
nor showing a desire to fight,
but indicating capability.

TWENTY FOUR

He who remains persevering
in danger, is without blame.
Do not complain about this truth;
Enjoy the good fortune you still possess.

畐

PROGRESS

TWENTY FIVE

The wise students,
when they hear of the Tao,
carry it earnestly into practice.

The average students,
when they hear of the Tao,
think about it now and then.

The foolish students,
when they hear of the Tao,
laugh loudly.

If it were not for the laughter,
the Tao would not be what it is.

TWENTY SIX

If all your life
you remain with a clear conscience,
you need not fear
a knock at the door at midnight.

TWENTY SEVEN

The sage has no mind
of his own
but is aware
of the needs of others.

Be good to people
who are good.
To those who are not good
be also good.
Thus goodness is achieved.

Be sincere to those
who are sincere.
To people who are not sincere,
be also sincere.
Thus all shall be sincere.

TWENTY EIGHT

I will overcome pride with humility,
hate with love, selfishness with
generosity, excitement with calmness,
ignorance with knowledge, evil with
good, and my restlessness with
the peace of meditation.

Finding peace in meditation,
I shall find all things
that I craved.

Dragon Flame (p. 121)
The symbolic gesture of palms out
means giving unto others of yourself.
Palms inward means that you are
retaining your powers.

TWENTY NINE

Overcome by yielding;
Unbend by being upright;
Be full by being empty;
Be new by wearing out;
Gain by having little;
Be confused by having much.

THIRTY

If someone is not as he should be
He has misfortune
And it does not further him
To undertake anything

THIRTY ONE

It is easier to carry an empty vessel
than a full one.
If you oversharpen the blade,
its edge will soon blunt.
The possessor of a hall filled with gold
will not be able to protect it.
To bear wealth and titles arrogantly
will bring disaster.

When good service has led to fame,
it is time to follow the Tao
and retire into obscurity.

RESOLUTENESS

THIRTY TWO

A good man
is the teacher of a bad man.
A bad man
is in the care of a good man.
If the teacher is not respected,
and the student not cared for,
confusion will arise.

THIRTY THREE

Those who know the Tao
do not need to speak of it.

Those who are ever ready
to speak of it, do not know it.

In the light of the setting sun,

men either beat the pot and sing

or loudly bewail

the approach of old age.

What is the Tao?
The Tao is.

PROVERBS

If happiness is in your destiny,
you need not be in a hurry.

Disease can be cured;
fate is incurable.

The universe is ruled by
letting things take their course.
It cannot be ruled by interfering.

PROVERBS 2

Though you amass ten thousand pieces of silver,
at death you cannot take with you even a copper
penny.

A wise person makes his own decisions,
a weak one obeys public opinion.

Sufferance is equal to consent.

A word whispered in the ear
can be heard for miles.

Mischief results from
too much opening of the mouth.

When the blind lead the blind,
they will both fall into the water.

A ship can find support in water;
water can turn it over.

Ten thousand rivers flow into the sea;
the sea is never full.

The farmer hopes for rain;
the traveler hopes for good weather.

Beasts do not know their own strength;
Men do not know their own faults.

Is there a person
who has not made one error
and half a mistake?

When you sit alone,
meditate on your faults.
In conversation,
do not discuss the faults of others.

PROVERBS 6

Remembering is for those
who have forgotten.

Wisdom is better than
weapons of war.

Over every possessor of knowledge
is one who is more knowing.

You may hide something from men;
you can hide nothing from the spirits.

If there is something that you don't
want anyone to know about,
don't do it.

A stupid man dies a stupid death.

PROVERBS 8

The tongue is soft and remains,
the teeth are hard and fall out.

When brothers and sisters argue,
the bystander takes advantage.

It is good to be neither high nor low.